MY SORE EYE'S

By Jerome K Godbee Jr

WWW.AVATARJR.NET

My Sore Eye's

ISBN 979-8-988 5325-0-7

Printed in the United States

TABLE OF CONTENTS

Chapter 1

Chapter 2

PREFACE

The way in which we respond to our life experiences sways the color of our souls, causing our energy to fluctuate up and down the light spectrum of our chakras. Some associate this with the idea of "going through the fire" and the outcome of these trials will reveal how we treat ourselves, our loved ones, and our acquaintances. This compilation of carefully chosen and newly created poems serves as an artful portrayal of my personal interpretation of a few of the moments in my life.

I was born in Harrisburg Pa. At the young age of 19, I was shot in the face, more specifically, directly in the mouth, following an argument during a house party. Years later, I joined a singing group and proved worthy enough to perform as the opening act for revered R&B vocalist Monica and Usher. Shortly after, I ventured into the arts, presenting my poetry at the Apollo Theatre, The Queen Latifa Show and multiple Radio performances Including Atlanta's V-103 station. I was cast in Tyler Perry's Why Did I Get Married too, The House of Payne and local Atlanta T.V. Series Misty as well as other roles in theater productions such as The Color Purple (B.I.D.H). amongst other works. I am grateful for these "relatively" joyful moments. But unfortunately, I got Married too quickly, and I found myself traversing the fire once again. *There are no poems contained within this book regarding my Marriage, for I revised this book in my present state of being, following my divorce,* embracing my condition and reviving my spirit to create once again. I was able to free myself from the years in which that relationship prevented me from producing even one word. Now, after emerging from the aftermath of this trial, the embers of a previous doctrine drifted away, revealing my true self and despite walking through the fire, and not being psychologically burned, I remain appreciative of being a loving soul.

Throughout my life experience, the spirit of my Ancestors was always with me, guiding me through the blinding light arriving here at this moment. It is interesting to look back and realize that I was always apprehensive about expressing my soul to others, fearing vulnerability. The streets have proven to be sticky, and we don't unlearn survival behavior as we grow older, but we adapt. Now I inner stand that we are all cosmically interconnected, with one spirit at the core of our existence, allowing us to relate and learn from our mutual experiences every day, so, it is my fervent wish from this work of art forward to continue to contribute to this connection, broadly articulating this life experience, now that I am a proper emotional man.

Enjoy,

Jerome k. Godbee Jr

My will desired life

so, my spirit began a whirlwind

and like the sun

my soul

made my voice

a symbol

of care and power.

CHAPTER 1

Love and Pain

Life is love
reflected from the sun's affection
and the moon blushes
intimate thoughts of you
then the ocean began
to ripple waves
and waves of passionate dreams
and the tides overflow

everything inside love
is unbelievable

caterpillars become butterflies by
preconceiving
your inner heart desires
you're that blue fire
in the bitter cold
and that bold untainted power
resides in your soul
a haven where infatuations unfold
a place where babies grow
where every truth is told
where a simple kiss
can be incredible

your lust takes
philosophies for hostages
your rage
is the balance of your kind self
your sorrows
are the shadows of god
and if could speak
would prove itself sweeter
than joy

without sorrows

I ... *would have never known*
happiness

without Joy

I... would have never learned
from my mistakes

Love is pain.

American Made

These two worlds of mine
are about to collide
and in between them is my gift
I don't know how long
I will survive this street life
so, I continue to be thankful
for everything
and especially for a good soul
and grateful to be wise
and just as strong as a devil

for peace sake
I studied the ways
of the peace makers
embracing the fact
that heroes are killers too

ambitious men and women
eager to pledge themselves
gamble with their lives
crafting surreptitious methods
to send souls back
from which they came
before knowledge of themselves
can be attained
in the name of national security

I can say I loved hard
once in this life
and I learned

that love
is being able to con someone
into stupidity

I'm not nice

I'm not one of those... gentlemen
I live in a privileged power
of the poor and the rich
and spiritual deception
is the cornerstone of its strength
and among them
exposing the moral position
is a hostile attack on their image
and so...
like a broken-hearted child
I adapt
to whatever that experience
means
to my mind

I'm surrounded by gangsters,
police, politicians, secret societies
and the papacy, *who furtively*
stalk fearless men and women
who has lost their egos

the precursor in the vanguard of
moral mind power

I'm in intellectually deep

I am a captured black hole
with a library and a gun

just as the child is the reflection
of their parents
I am the reflection of society
that... American baby boy

I am a brilliant shadow
and within my presence
a constant frightening pleasure
remains
rippling the perception
of unconstitutional reverence

depending on the second, minute
and the hour
I am many beautiful experiences
and the nightmare

I am a man phased

I loved my life as a child
reckless with it
when I was young
comprehend it now that I'm older

born to cabal in these streets
socially bred to mistrust
the authority
that covertly
provides me with the means
to be a fugitive spirit
or an order taking subdued idol
causing **or** defending the chaos
technocratically hypnotized
to constantly awake
in an organized living hell
and its ruthless heaven
and trauma bonded
to defend its duality

and so...

I bravely select *my implied choice*

between the hammer
and the anvil

given by the imperial mute avatar
of Uncle Sam

the manner of death

for being born in this system

I am MADE

in

AMERICA.

The Great Reset

I asked the Sun
would it give its life for you?
and it said:
if she were mine

yes

there would be no more light

I asked the Moon
would it ever lie for you?
and it said:

yes

I will say it with a straight face
and truly believe?
that what I am saying
is right

I asked the Rain
if she had broken its heart
how would it respond?
and the Rain said:

the fragility and contrast
intrigues my journey through her

I'll Rain
for planetary days
upon planetary nights

as you are *omniscient*
all mighty... living

VAULT

she is...
different...

would you be
overprotective of her?

and the Vault spoke:

she is... your *passion*
therefore
my creation as well

and so...

I will choose to... ***forgive***

and I will not kill the Sun
nor decapitate the Moon
or murder the Rain
for their youthful curiosity

but... *I will **seize** her*

and rest within its meaning

be...

and *dream...*

dream of lacking empathy
& compassion

to manipulate, possess
and control

to be malevolent

for I am all experiences

and when I rise
from my beautiful nightmare

so, will this creation
absorb within me

and the spirit of love will flourish
as always.

<u>The Joyful Throe of Attachment</u>

I miss hugging you
I miss kissing you

I miss holding your sexy body

I miss the laughing

your moaning
how you smell

your groaning

I miss everything about you

and I want some more

I need some more

hurry home

it's cold

I'm

Missing... you.

4u

Every time the sun shines
and every time it rains
everything grows a little more
each day

when babies are born
another star begins to be
the moon smiles
and the comets fly by to see

life is so beautiful
and it's what you make it

another year older is a blessing
wisdom grows with age
keep your head up always
because you are that shining star
live right and be strong

be divine
and never cease to expand
your infinite mind
you are a goddess
a living queen of the earth
and glory belongs to you
whether your conscience
remembers
or not

so, with my highest respect

I thank you for this experience

that's why I wrote this poem

4u.

<u>Divinity</u>

It's cool and quiet
and I feel so alone
I'm there watching the stars
evolve in awe
counting the millenniums
in a glorious kingdom
with no windows or doors

then I saw love and trust
riding on the outstretched arms

of an angel of divine beauty
the most beautiful entity
I ever seen
pauses 3 inches from my face
vibrating

veins avec moi je un cadeau pour
toi

that whisper was indescribable

it spoke to my gene
the feeling was immense
blending into oneness
it was life beyond this dimension

my physical right then exploded

bursting!

spreading light to everything
known

I woke suddenly half blind
unstable
and confused

and withdrew
like a heroin addict

I looked upon myself amazed
at what I had seen

**it was heaven
in its physical form**

on top of me
loving me
in multiple motions

now ultimately realizing
I was in between a dream
and a physical dream

sweating profusely
my heart racing
I'm tingly and drained
the blessing was two-fold

I grabbed her thighs
as I closed my eyes
and shed a tear
for pleasure

her soft wet womb
moaned love songs

and I was the jazz man
constantly
changing
that rhythm!
oh!

I remember the moonlight
bouncing off her wet brown skin
and her making chronic
angelic tones
she couldn't restrain
she took me to a place

and *brought me back!?*

do these women truly know
the powers they possess?

whoa

my wifey caught me by surprise
twinkled my brown eyes

then she quietly gazed
my facial features
and slowly licked her lips

tells me

that, ***she loves me***

kisses me

and say's

good night.

<u>My breath doesn't stink, I look good and I got on good smelling cologne</u>

You looked so beautiful today
and then I mustard up the courage
to speak to you
is it just me
or do you feel the same way
intimacy dances in our air
and I swear
I can smell your affections
and I can just taste

your inner thoughts
and I've been trying
to hold my breath
in your presence but I cannot
and my heart continues
to skip and burn
and my skin begins
to weep and yearn

my attraction to you
is as the oceans is to the moon
creating a million ripples
in my mental
when I see you

and I start to imagine your hugs
are as warm as the sunrays
and as soft as cotton candy

I'm stealing
your chocolate kisses now
making you happy

seven days, three hours, sixteen
minutes
and eight seconds

and I know if I had the chance
to really get to know you
you could bend my will
at your discretion

my love is a *part* of your
imagination

it rests on the ocean floors

the reality of it awaits
at the fingertips
of your hands and mine
with the softest kiss ever
momentarily pausing time
you see baby
my words run with the wind
and I just can't hold them in
it's like trying to stop the waters
from smoothing out the sand
like the finest red oak in the land
my heart stands
strong, vibrant, grounded
and my mind ripples again

observing the heat in my hands

I see you now loving me
with all your might!

I feel the winds compassion
and I see
every tear dancing for us

seven days, three hours, sixteen
minutes
and eight seconds

you had me

open

imagining what it would be like

being with you

fantasizing

about the most interesting
conversation

ever

making your energy aware

that we could

possibly be

soul mates

instead of you...

you...　　　　just...

walking

away quickly after I said
how you doing what's your...

CHAPTER 2

<u>Loves Energy</u>

She felt the inner most part of me
my life
and all that I want to be
my words became hers that day
in a place between time and space

and we had become one
as I spoke and she listened
as I sung and she cried

it was beautiful
this synergy of affection
hearing the tears falling
from her eyes

how empathetic

how compassionate

and entwined

two hearts can be

right then
she knew me
emotionally
that bond
that last
eternally

she felt what God gave us
reverberate

she felt... *our soul...*

tie.

When The Lion Roars

When it rains
when it snows
when it's hot
when it's cold
I'll be loving you

when you're happy
when you're sad
when you're funny
when you're mad

I'll be there

when I say I love your eyes
when I say I love your smile
when I say I love your body
when I say you're beautiful
trust my truth

when I say I am
when I say ready
when I say for your
when I say love

just give it to me.

What I Love About You

I love it so much
when you hold me in your arms
it's the softness of your skin
the pillows of your breast
it's the feeling of being cared for
is what I love the best

I love it so much
when you're being sexy
it's how you slide your genes on
it's how you rub on my head

and talk spoiled
when you want something girl
it's the way you lay on my chest
after sex
making me feel like a hero
yea
that's what I love

I love it so much
when you dance alone
it's the way
you look me in my eyes
while you slow grind
making my emotions erect
girl you got me waiting to exhale
taking in long deep breaths

it's how provocative
and passionate you can be

it's how you *mentally tease me*

yea baby... that's what I love about
you.

Guardian Angels

A man can make his stand but
a woman makes a stronger man
I must surrender to my better self
and be the divine being that I am
living in today's patriarch society
I need you beside me
for your emotional

intellectual, and psychological
support
keeping me balanced and happy
in my thoughts

and side-by-side

we will grow to be selfless
and I swear to protect you
by any means

divine she is and all should know
that women
are guardian angels.

The Involuntary Spirituality
of Now

I free fell intensely
my vulnerability came too
I tried to spread my wings
but selective memories of her
overwhelmed my being
and those intensified
after thoughts

made my body weak
so, I descended steadfast
into my insecurities
suffocating in my denial
and jealousy was preparing me
to hit rock bottom.

I opened the door to our home
and there were her panties
lying on the floor
my adrenaline started to flow
we've played games
like this before
her spontaneous ways
are blessings
she must have saw me
coming home
though the window

her ability to be provocative
simply makes my soul feel happy

so, in the living room
I took off all my clothes
except my socks
because I don't like

when my feet get cold

I'm going to give my angel
everything she's been waiting for
as I creep up the stairs
I hear our favorite song
and my stomach
flutters a moment

remembering our bond
now my superpower knows
exactly
where the music is coming from

as I got close to her
Victoria secret bra
hanging off a picture frame
on the wall

I heard a moan
that seems to seep
through the cracks
of our bedroom door

I stopped!

anticipation had me thinking
to myself
I said **damn?!**
she started pleasing herself
she's ready

mentally she provoked an image
that aroused my big brown cock
and she was doing it
because she knew I like to watch
the bedroom door was open
but where did she go?
then I heard her voice
helplessly catch its breath
it echoed off the bathroom walls
the playful freak that I am
I got on my knees
and placed my good eye
to the floor

her hand was trying grip
the black tiles
I recognized the diamond ring
I bought for her
along with someone else's knee
and elbow?!

I arose up off the floor

my mind is blank
my mind is blank

I walked downstairs
and got the **butcher's knife**
out of our kitchen drawer

my mind is blank
my mind is blank

and there I was standing
in front of the bathroom door
I love this woman with all my soul
I'm a Sagittarius
and all I could focus on
was killing this man
and the woman I still love

I knocked the hinges off the door
because I kicked it
with an outer body
uncontrollable rage
my face changed

and I screamed!!!
like the beast I became

AH!!!

and I raised that 13-inch knife
and before I struck them both
sending us all to hell!
my face refashioned itself...

it was our **neighbor?**

the 28-year-old beauty... queen...
girl... successful...

it was **Samone?**

and her face was in a place
where mine belonged

they screamed
a quick ear popping horror
in shock I dropped the knife

the moment paused time
then we fast-forwarded

all of us were out of breath
and dumb founded

all eyes wide open I Stoddard
what the ffffbabe umm...

the hair trigger intoxication
had me confused
and lost for words

then, *Samone*
bloomed a fearfully kind, breathy
erotic, fetish sound

what happens now?

I didn't answer the question
my wifey eyes moaned a smile
my body overheated instantly
when I heard Samone's saliva
cracking in her mouth
as she licked her lips afterwards
and there I was standing
in the doorway butt naked

their eyes on my full erection

as it mimicked my heartbeat

our unvoiced expressions
leaked...
heavy...

Samone bent down
and kissed
the top of my right foot

my wife to be
reached out for my hand
and euphoria seized
my nervous system

and I stepped *forward*
like a wild 200 pound
newborn beast
taking a step for the first time

and love, rage, lust, and fear
were *seduced*

instantaneously

our speaking voices flooded

from eagerly test tasting
our blended flesh

we became naturally high

freely jubilating
in our ***right now***
deeply inhaling
the potent source of creation

perpetually **exhaling**

our

vocal

frenzy.

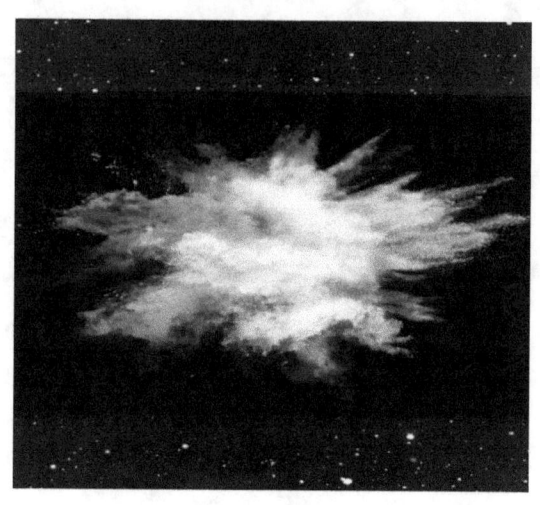

<u>Nocturnal Emissions</u>

Love dreams
how erotic
spontaneous and passionate
they can be
the perfect dream
sexy scenes
outside
on top of a 200-story building
surrounded by our most
intimate desires
and only

the clouds and the sun
can see
the super woman
she's giving to me

and when I awake
from my one-night fantasy
I wonder do I move
the way I move
in my dreams

do I moan and grunt?
hug sheets and pillows
because it feels so good to me

do I call out her name? if not
what do I say?

my thoughts of lust
constantly eagers to play

but on the dreamy side of things

and this will always be

I never liked waking up

sticky.

<u>The Day Song</u>

The day I fall in love
will be the happiest day of my life
the sun will shine for us
and the rain will glow
and her love will fall from the sky
from a rainbow
into my life

the day it rains
when I fall in love
when the sun shines

and the rainbow comes
you'll know that another true love
is born.

<u>Is Possible</u>

Loving you
could be more beautiful
than the sight of sunrays
bathing on top of the sea

more refreshing
than a gust of cold air
at 110 degrees
love me

religiously

the same way my lungs are in love
with the air we breathe

the same way my eyes loves to see
and my mind loves to think

love me and hold me
as if you thought I returned
to the essence
and seeing me again
was a blessing
and let's kiss
and let the sight of our passion
contagious

and if this land
of un healing hearts
acts a bit afraid to catch it

you fear not

because *I swear,* I will love you
as unpredictable as the waves
smoothing out the sand.

Being Pussy whipped can be intensely euphoric only if She is Dick whipped

From me to you
with all my love, trust
and honesty
I give you all that I am

from my heart to your heart
with loyalty and friendship

I promise to always respect
and protect you

from your soft brown lips
to mine
with much desire and sincerity
we will always kiss

and when every opportunity
we reach our blissful peak
we'll submit each other's minds
and bodies
as god intended
and make love as if we knew
we were dying tomorrow
through the night.

CHAPTER 3

<u>To Whom It May Concern</u>

To whom it may concern
I got shot in my mouth
and almost died
never to mature
from my selfish age
never to say again:
I'm not selling weed
out the house

you know I'm popular
people love me
out my young deceitful mouth

To whom it may concern

I've reflected some bad behaviors
that I've adsorbed
from my environment
don't be so eager to deem me
I was young and mentally lost
and
the wows of this life experience
happened because
It was exactly what was needed

To whom it may concern

I let no mankind
control my emotions
I am not the man I used to be
I've remembered to enjoy this life
but don't exceed in provoking me

To whom it may concern

I used to wonder
why it seems that
someone is always suffering
and then I thought?

if you believe it in your mind
and feel it in your heart
and believe it as if it is predestined
your mind will create
what you will it

To whom it may concern

I struggled a lifetime to unwind
and become a proper
emotional man
I absolutely envision
how Stevie can see
and as well
when Neo was approaching

The Machine City

free to follow my gut & brain
powers
free to trust the vibrations within
that timely informs me

that I've become...

enlightened

to whom it may concern.

The Flower of My Life

I fell in love
so deep in love
when the sun began to shine
and the hands of the rain
soothed my pain
falling from the radiant sky

universal energy's
forever loving me
unconditionally

nurturing me
that I may grow
strong and tall
benevolent and mighty
and beautiful

and when I began to know myself
the rogue was removed
from my eye
and when I realized the purpose
of my life
I cried
and cried

grateful tears for being
feeling all things in creation
that exists within me

and when I return to the essence

I'll still be in love

so deep in love

for eternity.

Street Life
song

Why do my eyes
hunger for the street life

ghetto fame

playing those deadly games
the only life I know
the only way I could survive
survive

I did what I had to do
wrong or right
living the street life

the effects of
growing up poor
will always be
apart of me
every time I open my eyes

but for me to survive
the street life
I gotta let it go.

<u>A Mothers Love</u>
song

We started out
with just the clothes on our backs
we had it hard growing up
so hard
but *Momma* you seem
to come through
for us
when there was no way no how

we were blessed
because you made the ways
Momma
to get us through the days
you were strong
before we knew what it was

a Mothers love
is unconditional
it falls like rain
into our souls
a Mothers love
is like no other
so, thank God for her
thank you, Grandma and Grandpa.

Good Times

Remember
when you kept asking me
what were the fruits of the spirit?
and I kept saying: yea? Mom?
(like... why wouldn't I know
the name of fruits?)

and I kept oddly gazing
and chanting:

orange... apples... pears...
bananas... peaches...

I didn't understand
why I was so funny
until you explained to me
the churches philosophy
all I knew was that it was always
good
to see you laugh

remember when I poured
3 long goops of hot sauce
down Minister Briggmans throat
when he fell asleep with his
mouth open *on our couch*

300 + pounds chased
me around the house
he tried to get me
he was **mad?!**
he probably thought
he was in hell for a second

remember the times when you
you... used to come to the hospital

just to massage my feet
I was paralyzed
and I couldn't walk at the time
I couldn't feel it
but it sure *did feel good*
Mom... when I was *good* and *bad*
you were *always* there for me

remember when Starkeisha and I
left for school
then came back home
5 minutes later
with baby diarrhea poop

ALL OVER US!

she cried like a grown woman
at 8 years old

she hit me in the head with that
soft white plastic bag **TWICE I**

and she wouldn't stop playing
around chasing me with it

so... *I took it from her*
and I beat her with it

who knew?

not us

remember when you
you... kicked me out the house
and I moved next door
for three weeks
all because of Naja's
academy award performance

she charged at me
like a raging rhinoceros!

I stiffed armed her

and she *performed*

in the end, I got it, **I was wrong**

but you knew you missed me
(smile)

I missed you more

we all know

there's no place like home

Good times.

Unity

I had broken my leg
when I was young
and my mother cried

and my sisters cried

and Keisha cried

and Miss Carry cried

and Mack cried
and Kandy just starred
but I could tell she cared
and some people laughed
most tried to imagine the pain
my foot was facing the wrong way
I remember that day
when my family and friends
had cried
and then *I started to cry*
it was **beautiful**

you may forget the ones whom
you laugh with

but never the ones
whom you cry with.

Dedicated to: 5th & Woodbine

My Melody

when I sing

dogs howl

rooster's cockle doodle doo

flowers bloom
people stop in their tracks

people go

the sun rises

the rivers flow
the moon shines

people laugh
people smile

sometimes cry
the world turns

the wind blows

legends fall
stars are born

people stare

people feel me
people have sex

and I laugh

sometimes I get emotional
but it is *my greatest strength*

I'm sad at moments
and then I'm happy

I'm judging myself to hard I stop

and then I go ahead
and cheer myself on

I love my voice

no matter what anybody says

I am happy

when I sing.

Rain Therapy

Like a child who sees his mother
stretching forth her arms
I am compelled
to walk into the rain

this...

is nature's physical manifestation

calling to embrace
my organic machine

as the rain down pours
on top of me
stripping the future man taught
instinct to run for shelter

I am gradually consoled
as it innately
hushes my human issues

a dormant healing gene
embedded
in my DNA awakens

I feel, *safe*

there is something sacred
about this

a rainy days worth is a jewel
for the body and soul
to experience

l am... *better*

I feel

lightened

if I cried right now
on this crowded street
no one would be able
to tell the difference

I have the overwhelming feeling
that absolutely nothing

in this world

could possibly love me more... than

water.

CHAPTER 4

I Be Dark Matter

I am
and I stir souls in a big black
Wizards pot
that is filled to the very rim
with my enchanting words
that at times overflows
and touches the fire below
evolves into steam
and blesses the air you breath

it is... I

and I am a *part* of your oneness
loving you from the core
of my mind
I am that *essence* that massages
the center of your *belly*
when your emotions become
overwhelmed
by repetitious intensified
after thoughts

I dwell in a place
where the bees
are the size of eagles
and the eagles
are the color of butterflies
I am a king

I am a king with [00] crowns
behold oo souls
oo stories untold
I don't he my eyes are as bright as
the muddy waters of little Egypt
reflecting the moons pale light
hypnotizing

the peery in your being

I am the Creators creation
and all I can comprehend
right now... is love

my love
lingers on the edge of your hopes
and my soul dances to the rhythm
of intimacy in your hearts
it moans the earths
gravitational pull
and emit large white puffy clouds
right now
I bless, thank,
and receive every thought

and every feeling unto you and I
and bless these atoms
and bless these molecules
for access

letting me know that I am an
infinite being
and not confusing me

I am telling you
we will never be alone

this world is our throne
and the copious universes
are our kingdoms

we are, immeasurable.

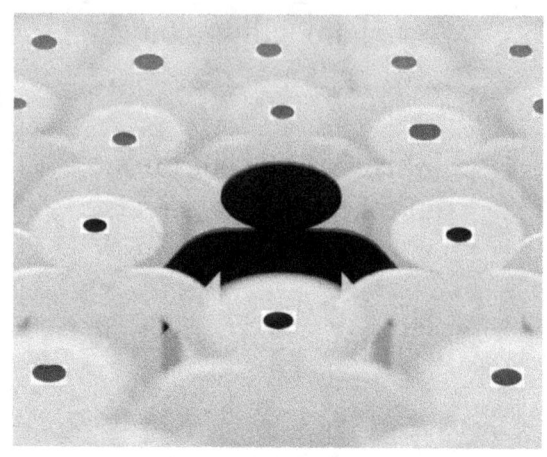

The Multidimensional Player

I was born at all times
it is not where I am from
or where I am at
it's *what I am*
because no matter what I achieve
how much I succeed or fail
I will always be

a devil the eyes of some

a god in the eyes of others

an immortal spirit to wise men

and a fool

to more than I like to imagine

and so...

I'll continue to dig graves...

preach...

that the **imagination**
is more **important**
than knowledge

I

will

infinitely

forever be

a **dream master.**

We Different

When we learn from our mistakes
we grow
when we hate it hinders the soul
and when we cry
the pain slowly falls

I really thought
my brown skin didn't count

when we use our minds
we accomplish great things

when we don't
like sheep we'll follow the Devil
appearing like God
straight into different hells

WHAT A COLD-BLOODED SCENE

creating ghettos in every
city was so mean?
convincing the controllers
that uplifting
the poor will only make us
a greater country
will outright be against their will

but with a lil multicultural
awareness
some historical research
and bravery

like no other land mass
we will reap the value
and power of our vote
and bargain for our specific best
interests

and as *one nation* we will flourish
and be free to guide
noble characters
to a higher form of humanity

they cannot rule as their
forefathers did

be different.

<u>Jack in the Box</u>

When I am happy
you are silly
when I am hurting
you are angry
when I'm feeling good
you're just fine
when I cry
you don't
when I'm sad
you isolate
when I am brave
you lack the courage
when I feel for another's pain

you conceal the sympathy

well... Jack.... Jack...

Yes?

we don't conceal sympathy
or lack courage nor isolate
or cry
but we... *observe*
all these complex frequencies
because "it is" the *lesson*
of this life
and to be able to see,
listen, and interpret
our heavy human experience
cosmically affirms we are back
on the right path
because only the balancing of
these energies will move us
forward on our journey
that's my voice?
yes... it is us
stepping outside of the box
now walk away.

<u>Earth</u>

I hear what's inaudible to man
and I discern what some men
cannot inner stand

if it is up to me
I would pluck away the sun
and shine in its place
I would shove the milky ways
and black holes somewhere
in the corner of space
and blow away the nearest

planets and moons

pardon me
please

for thinking so selfish

but

our plane

is just so beautiful.

Annie Get Your Gun

There is a war on women sports
and your true enemies
are elite men and women

I sense...
men are unapologetically
deeply chanting

Anything she can do
I can do better

wishful men that *only feel*
like women

aggressively protected
by sociopathic media
are obliterating your athletic
achievements
in a coup attempt too artfully
emotionally
intimidate your brave spirit
kill your ambition
and have you question
your reality

I will bet a water tower
of testosterone
that these men be chanting
after each meet

Anything she can do
I can do better

when they are alone
the same as when white people
say nigga
when by themselves

It's not a pleasant feeling
competing with super kind men
with the height and wingspan
comparable to Michael Phelps
damn

Anything she can do
I can do better

Uh...

and say something moral, truthful,
or fair
like:
men cannot have babies

and jack-eyed hypervigilant
spin techs on standby
will end your career
licking to distort
your human ethic

gang gang

swallow the pool water
and throw up your tears
in the locker room

war

Annie You Better.

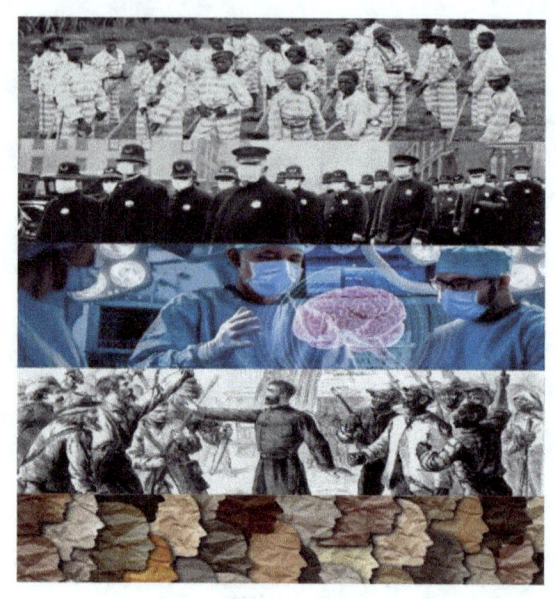

My Sore Eyes

I blinked my eyes
and there stood my brother

I blinked my eyes again
and there stood my sister

I blinked a third time
and there stood
a white man and a white woman

I dared not to blink again

I raised my arms
out in front of me
for the first time

they were a beautiful
mechanical design

suddenly etheric pressure
began to fill the seat to my soul

with a key
intuitively manifesting a sword
and shield

this life experience is
a United State

arriving at an age where
the mighty few rules
by compassionate manipulation
and politicians & entertainers
manage men

and women with fear
false kindness
and love for one another

history made up, dug up
covered up
or destroyed were the procedures

remember the time
when the only descriptions
pushed of Ethiopia
were the images of flies walking
on little brown children's eyes

that do not blink

My sore eye

constructed the old world
right here on the America's
and helped build
the modern cities
and win the wars

and *still* his wicked character
unashamed arrogance claimed
credit for culture, architecture
and ideas that wasn't his

and only when he's taking his
placebo constitutional moral meds
my brother *may* remember
to treat me fair

he knows me better
than I know my lower self
and willfully conceals my divinity

not by OUR choice
the welfare of neuro melanin
is not abundant in him

as it is in nature
and throughout the universe

and so...
for my brother
and his mighty few

cognitive dissonance... *bred
rejection*
instead of *honor*
and self-importance, enmity,
and disbelief
consumed his apparent
fragile reality

and...

I will never forget
his composure with Tuskegee

I will never forget
his malevolent heart
in Rosewood

I will never forget
his envious mind
to **bar** financial independence
in Tulsa Oklahoma

I will never forget
the decision they made
to put *us* in a box
and **covertly** *emotionally abuse us*

and *then accuse us*
of our condition

my nature had forgiven him

but only
through intense study of myself

and I pitied the both of us

the moment I inner stood
his mutation

before...

I trusted and believed
my brothers every word
and
marveled at his monetary
achievements

based on my moral

now...

I am astute to the mystery

of my side of OUR family's
abrogation
and wise enough to know
when in his presence
to ***pay attention***

so...

these days I'll give it a go
with patience

with **my *gun on my hip***

as our housefly
walks across my eye
as I interpret *the news*

*as I would a **personality disorder***

and don't blink

My sore eye's

About the Author

When a bullet struck him directly in the mouth at just 19 years of age, Jerome's life was forever changed. He refused to be held back by any limitations. Instead, he allowed the experience to propel him forward, strengthening his will, and is now a testament to the resilience of the human spirit.

Years later, he joined a R&B singing group and proved worthy to be the opening act for famous musical Artists Monica and Usher. Pursuing the arts further, Jerome was cast in the musical The Color Purple and Tyler Perry's movie Why Did 1 Get Married Too and more.

These new and selected poems reveal the universal truths woven into the fabric of his life. He invites the readers into the world of his heart, where they can explore their own inner light and embrace the power of the imagination.

This collection is not just poetry, but it offers a heavy symbiotic experience that box braids childhood memories, social issues, spirituality, and relationships. Through Jerome's evocative verses, readers are stirred to embrace a life filled with gratitude, courage, and love.